Living for Love

CW00382654

Living for Love
Selected Texts
Brother Roger of Taizé

1915–2005

Les Presses de Taizé

Contents

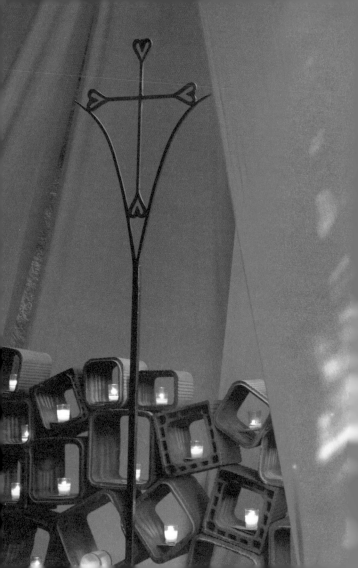

HERE ARE SOME PAGES that reveal the life and thought of Brother Roger. They present some texts by him, excerpts from his numerous writings collected under the titles of his principal books.

The legacy he left is alive. He had a conviction: God is united to every human being, even to those who are unaware of it. In this confidence in God's presence, he found a peace he sought to communicate to others.

Trust in God gave him the courage often to anticipate the movement of history. He opened ways forward where others could not see any. And he did so both to foster reconciliation among Christians as well as to contribute to peace in the human family.

He was aware of the great upheavals that would profoundly change our societies. He saw very early that modernity would make it difficult to trust in God; he understood those who were beset by doubts.

But he was not afraid of new developments. On the contrary, scientific discoveries passionately interested him and awakened in him the hope of improving the living conditions of the most destitute.

His attention to young people often led him to repeat: "I would go to the end of the earth if I could, to express over and over again my confidence in the younger generations."

His death remains a mystery. All his life he felt painfully the suffering of the innocent. And then, by a violent and senseless death, he himself joined those innocent.

Like John the Baptist, Brother Roger did not want to be at the centre himself; he wanted to point to Christ, to help people discover the presence of God. By his life and his death, he told us clearly that God's love was boundless and that everyone's calling was to live for love.

BROTHER ALOIS

Living Today for God

WILL YOU WELCOME each new day as God's today? In every season, will you find ways of discovering life's poetry, on days full of light as well as in winter's frozen nights? Will you discover how to bring joy to your humble dwelling by small signs that cheer the heart?

GATHER EVERYTHING that happens, trivialities included, without reservation, regret or nostalgia, in inexhaustible wonder. Set out, going forward one step at a time, from doubt towards faith, not worrying about the impossible ahead. Light fire, even with the thorns that tear you.

FROM THE TIME of the apostles, the Virgin Mary and the first believers, there has been a call to live in great simplicity and to share. One of the pure joys of the Gospel is to go further and further toward a simplicity of heart that leads to a simplicity of living.

Simplifying never means choosing an ice-cold austerity, without kind-heartedness, filled with judgements upon those who do not take the same road. If simplicity of life became equated with gloom, how could it lead us to the Gospel? The spirit of simplicity shines through in signs of serene joy, and also in cheerfulness of heart. Simplifying invites us to arrange what little we have in creation's simple beauty.

SIMPLIFYING OUR LIVES enables us to share with the least fortunate, to alleviate suffering where there is disease, poverty, famine....

Our brothers in Taizé, as well as those living on other continents among the very poor, are keenly aware that we are called to a simple life. We have discovered that it does not keep us from offering hospitality day after day.

God of all mercy, you bury our past in the heart of Christ and you are going to take care of our future.

The Dynamic of the Provisional

THINGS ARE MOVING faster today than ever before. Only by living the dynamic of the provisional can we discover how, time after time, to keep on gaining new momentum. This will leave us free to advance – and we are all the freer, the more faithful we are to what is essential.

WHOEVER IS ON A JOURNEY towards God goes from one beginning to another beginning. Will you be among those who dare to tell themselves: "Begin again! Leave discouragement behind! Let your soul live!"

IT MUST BE SAID that only someone with a sense of continuity can benefit from the dynamic of the provisional.

Enthusiasm, fervour, is a positive force, but it is by no means enough. It burns itself out and vanishes if it does not transmit its momentum to another force, deeper and less perceptible, which enables us to keep on going our whole life long. It is indispensable to ensure continuity, for times of enthusiasm alternate with periods of lifelessness, arid deserts.

So it is with regularity in prayer. One day, the regularity and the continuity will be the springboard for a new leap forward.

PEOPLE

ndLiche

Joves

처녀

ㅇ

МолодЕжи

ES

EMPF
AUF DE

WELC
EN

IF SPIRITUAL VALUES in many countries were not being called into question, our community would not be setting in motion a whole process that consists in welcoming, week after week, young people not just from the North, East and South of Europe, but also from other continents.

Seeing all these faces on our hill of Taizé, we realize that they come with vital questions: What does Christ want from me? How can I find a meaning for my life in him? Without always sensing it clearly, they are trying to follow Christ. The important thing for my brothers and myself is to respond to their trust by being above all men of prayer and of listening, never spiritual masters.

Holy Spirit, enable us to bring peace into places of opposition, and to make visible by our lives a reflection of God's compassion. Yes, enable us to love and to express it by our lives.

Festival Without End

IF FESTIVITY WERE TO VANISH from people's lives.... If we were to awake one fine morning, in a society that was well organized, functional and contented – but devoid of any spontaneity....

If Christians' prayer were to become a sheer intellectual exercise, so secularized as to have lost all sense of mystery and poetry, with no place for the body to pray, no room for intuitions or for the affections....

If festivity faded away from the body of Christ, the Church, where on earth could there still be found a place of communion for the whole of humankind? It is thirst for communion that I sense in the young people here on the hill. For them, as for every generation, it is strong to the point of anguish. Communion with others in their struggles and aspirations, although these are years that are witnessing a crisis of confidence in humanity. Communion with Christ.

If the festival within me faded out, would I still have the energy to keep searching, ever anew, for communion with the rising generations?

THROUGHOUT YOUR DAY let work and rest be quickened by the Word of God. Keep inner silence in all things and you will dwell in Christ. Be filled with the spirit of the beatitudes: joy, simplicity, mercy.

HAPPINESS: there it is, within reach. Never seek it; it would only flee. It lies in attentiveness and in wonder. Happiness seems sometimes to disappear for a long, long time. And yet there it is, when eyes meet.

God of mercy, we are yearning for peace of heart. And the Gospel allows us to glimpse that, even in hours of darkness, you love us and you want happiness for us.

Struggle and Contemplation

STRUGGLE AND CONTEMPLATION: two poles between which we are somehow to situate our whole existence?

IN PRAYER OR IN STRUGGLE, only one thing is disastrous, the loss of love.

Do you see? Struggle and contemplation arise from the very same source, Christ who is love. If you pray, it is out of love. If you struggle to restore dignity to the exploited, that too is for love. At the risk of losing your life for love, will you live Christ for others?

IF SOME ARE GRIPPED by worry about the future and find themselves at a standstill, there are also young people all over the world who are inventive and creative. They know that God did not create us to be passive. For them, life is not subject to a blind destiny. They are aware that scepticism and discouragement have the power to paralyze human beings.

It is not only the leaders of nations who build the world of tomorrow. The most obscure and humble people can play a part in bringing about a future of peace.

In human beings there can be impulses to violence. For trust on earth we need to begin with ourselves, making our way forward with a reconciled heart, living in peace with those around us.

Peace on earth is prepared insofar as we dare to ask ourselves: Am I ready to seek inner peace and to go forward in selflessness. Even if I am empty-handed, can I be a ferment of trust in my own situation, understanding others more and more?

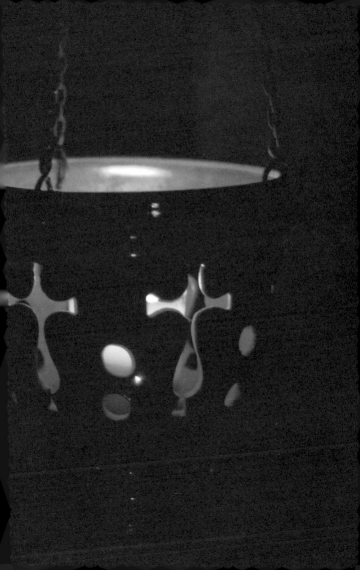

God of compassion, disconcerted by the incomprehensible suffering of the innocent, we pray for those who are experiencing times of trial. Inspire the hearts of those who seek the peace that is so indispensable for the whole human family.

A Life We Never Dared Hope For

FOR THOSE WHO RISK their whole lives, no road ever comes to a dead end. We think we have abandoned Christ, but he does not abandon us. We think that we have forgotten him, yet he was there. And we set out once more, we begin all over again, he is present. That is the unexpected; that is what we had not dared hope for.

FOR A LIFE TO BE BEAUTIFUL, it is not really necessary to have exceptional abilities or special skills: there is a happiness in giving oneself.

WHEN WE ARE FACED with the Gospel call to say yes for our entire lifetime, sometimes the question arises: "How can I remain faithful?" The yes fascinates, and at the same time it can frighten. And we hesitate. But one day we are astonished to find ourselves on the road, walking in Christ's footsteps: the yes had already been placed in the very depths of our being by the Holy Spirit. Then we begin to understand Mary's response: "May it be done to me according to your word."

HOW CAN I BE MYSELF? How can I fulfill myself? Those questions preoccupy some people to the point of anguish. When the Gospel asks people to be themselves and develop their gifts and talents a hundredfold, it is not in order to serve their own ends. It is to serve others.

In the Gospel, to be oneself means searching deeply until the irreplaceable gift given to each one of us is revealed. So keep silence, withdraw into the desert, if only once in a lifetime, and discover that gift.

Christ Jesus, like some of your disciples,
we sometimes find ourselves struggling to
understand your risen presence. But by your
Holy Spirit you live in us, and to each one
you say: "Come, follow me;
I have opened for you a way of life."

The Wonder of a Love

CHRIST, LOVE OF ALL LOVING, is a fire that burns within you. And when love is forgiveness, your heart, though tested, begins to live once more. The contemplation of his forgiveness becomes a radiant kindness in hearts that are simple. And the holiness of Christ is no longer out of reach.

WE ARE ASTONISHED by an unsuspected joy: the Holy Spirit wants to turn us into beings that are utterly transparent, like the sky on a spring day.

The Gospel bears within it such a radiant hope and such a call to joy that we would like to communicate them to people close at hand and far away, by going even to the point of giving ourselves.

Where is the source of hope and of joy? It is in God, who tirelessly seeks us out and finds in us the profound beauty of the human soul.

IT CAN HAPPEN that wonder at his love leads
you to say:

"This Jesus, the Risen Christ, was in me and yet I
felt nothing of his presence. So often I was looking
elsewhere for him. As long as I continued to run
away from the wellsprings he had placed in the
hollow of my being, I might well go far, very far, but
I kept getting lost on roads that led nowhere. There
seemed no way to find a joy in God.

"Then the time came when I realized that Christ had
never left me. I hardly dared speak to him, but he
understood, and already he spoke to me. When the
veil of worry was lifted, the trusting of faith came to
illuminate even my own night."

Jesus Christ, overwhelmed with trials, you
threatened no one; you forgave.
We too wish to know how to forgive
again and again.
That is the fullness of loving.

And Your Deserts Shall Flower

EVEN WHEN YOU CANNOT RECOGNIZE HIM, will you stay close to him in long silences when nothing seems to be happening? There, with him, life's most significant decisions take shape.

Tell him everything, and let him sing within you the radiant gift of life. Tell him everything, even what cannot be expressed and what is absurd.

In your struggles, he brings a few words, an intuition or an image to your mind ... And within you grows a desert flower, a flower of delight.

WE ARE IN A WORLD where light and darkness co-exist.

As we aspire to the light, could a doubt take hold of us? A Russian believer, Dostoyevsky, far from worrying about this, wrote, "I am a child of doubt and unbelief. What terrible suffering it has cost me and still costs me, this longing to believe, which is so much the stronger in my soul as more arguments against it rise up within me.... My 'hosanna' has passed through the crucible of doubt."

And yet Dostoyevsky could continue, "There is nothing more beautiful, more profound, more perfect than Christ. Not only is there nothing, but there can be nothing."

When that man of God suggests that the non-believer coexists in him with the believer, his passionate love for Christ still remains undiminished.

Happy are those who walk from doubt towards the brightness of a humble trusting in Christ! Just like the sun dispelling the morning mist, light will shine in the nights of the soul. Not an illusory trust but a clear-headed one, that impels us to act in the midst of real-life situations, to understand, to love.

Breath Of Christ's loving, breath of fire, kindle the deserts of our heart. Penetrate them through and through. Melt away all that rebels against the mystery of communion in you.

Peace of Heart in All Things

CONSENTING OVER AND OVER AGAIN to the trials that are so often part of human life. Searching for peace of heart in all things. And life becomes beautiful ... Yes, life will be beautiful. And then something we never dared hope for appears.

Christ knows what an inner combat we can sometimes wage in order to be found transparent. This struggle within is a sign of our love for him. But our life is not one of constant struggle. As we welcome the Gospel's message of joy, the Holy Spirit brings us what we often did not expect – peace of heart, and with it a happiness.

WITH YOUR HEART AT PEACE, your worries about yourself fade into thin air.

What matters most for you is discovering that God loves you. God's love is a presence; it is forgiveness. Peace of heart is possible, and even certain, because God's forgiveness radiates confidence.

God loves you even if you think you do not love God. And there will come a day when you will say to God: I love you, perhaps not as I would like to, but I do love you.

BY HIS HOLY SPIRIT, the Risen Christ penetrates, in order to transfigure it, even what is most disconcerting in you. All forms of pessimism that you harbour about yourself melt away. Away with those sombre impressions that your imagination can produce! And a peace of heart shines out.

Sing my soul: I belong to Christ; I am Christ's. An imperceptible inner transformation, the transfiguration of your being continues your whole life long. It allows you to live in the present moment; it makes each day God's own today. It is, already on this earth, the beginning of the resurrection, the dawning of the life that has no end.

Holy Spirit, consoling Spirit, when we remain in your presence, silent, at peace, that is already prayer. You understand everything about us, and at times even a simple sigh can be a prayer.

God Is Love Alone

IN HIS GOSPEL, in a dazzling intuition, Saint John expresses who God is in three words: "God is love." If we can grasp only those three words, we shall go far, very far.

What captivates us in those words? The fact that they transmit this luminous conviction: God did not send Christ to earth to condemn anyone, but for every human being to know that he or she is loved and to be able to find a road to communion with God.

KIND-HEARTEDNESS is not gullible; it requires us to be vigilant. It can lead us to take risks. It leaves no room for looking down on others. It makes us attentive to the most destitute, to the suffering of children. It lets us show with a look or a tone of voice that every human being needs to be loved.

Yes, God enables us to make our way forward with a spark of goodness in the depths of our souls, a spark that asks only to burst into flame.

WHY ARE SOME PEOPLE gripped by the wonder of a love and know that they are loved, or even cherished? Why do others have the impression that they are neglected?

If only everyone could realize that God remains alongside us even in the fathomless depths of our loneliness. God says to each person, "You are precious in my sight, I treasure you and I love you." Yes, all God can do is give his love; that sums up the whole of the Gospel.

God trusts us so much that he has a call for each one of us. What is that call? God invites us to love as he loves. And there is no deeper love than to go to the point of giving oneself, for God and for others.

God of Peace, you love and you seek out each one of us even before we loved you. And so we are filled with astonishment to discover that you look at every human being with infinite tenderness and deep compassion.

IF WE COULD ALWAYS REMEMBER that Christ is communion....

He did not come to earth to start one more religion, but to offer to all a communion in God. His disciples are called to be a humble leaven of trust and peace within humanity.... "Communion" is one of the most beautiful names of the Church.

THE DAILY ASPIRATION of my brothers and myself is for every young person to discover Christ, not Christ taken in isolation, but the "Christ of communion" present in fullness in that mystery of communion which is his Body, the Church. There many of the young can find a place to commit their whole lives to the very end. There they have all they need to become creators of trust, of reconciliation, not just among themselves but together with all the generations.

We would go to the ends of the earth to look for ways, to ask, to call, to implore if need be, but never from the outside, always while remaining within that unique communion which is the Church.

WHEN TIRELESSLY THE CHURCH LISTENS, heals and reconciles, it becomes what it is at its most luminous – a communion of love, of compassion, of consolation, a limpid reflection of the Risen Christ. Never distant, never on the defensive, freed from all forms of severity, the Church can let the humble trusting of faith shine right into our human hearts.

NEVER RESIGN YOURSELF to the scandal of the separation of Christians, all so readily professing love for their neighbour, yet remaining divided. Make the unity of Christ's Body your passionate concern.

Holy Spirit, you fill the universe, and you cause a life of communion with God to grow within each one of us.
And there, goodness of heart and self-forgetting for the sake of others burst into flower.

Chronology of Brother Roger's Life

1915	May 12, born in Provence (Switzerland), ninth child of Charles Schutz and Amélie Marsauche.
1931	Ill with pulmonary tuberculosis for several years.
1936–1939	Studies theology at Lausanne and Strasbourg.
1939	Becomes president of the Christian Student Association in Lausanne.
	Creates a group of young people who meet to share and for retreats.
1940	Leaves for France as World War II begins. Arrives in Taizé on August 20. Welcomes refugees, especially Jews.
1942	While visiting Geneva, learns that the occupation police has found out about him and that he cannot return to Taizé. Begins a life of community in Geneva with the first three brothers.

1944	The four return to Taizé to live. They welcome German prisoners-of-war, and take charge of twenty children orphaned by the war.
1949	The first seven brothers commit themselves for life to living together in great simplicity. Brother Roger is the prior of the community.
	First trip to Rome; audience with Pope Pius XII.
1951	When the community numbers twelve brothers, some are sent to share the life of the poorest, first in a nearby city, later on other continents.
1952–1953	Composes the "Rule of Taizé".
1958	First meeting with Pope John XXIII. From that time on, Brother Roger will have yearly meetings with John XXIII, Paul IV and John Paul II.
1960/1961	Catholic bishops and Protestant pastors are invited to spend three days in Taizé. First meeting of this kind since the sixteenth century.

1962	February, in Constantinople, visit to the Orthodox Patriarch Athenagoras.
	On the way back, first visit to Eastern Europe (Bulgaria and Yugoslavia). Brother Roger will return often before the fall of the Berlin Wall (Poland, East Germany, Hungary, Czechoslovakia, Russia, Romania).
	August, inauguration of the Church of Reconciliation.
	October, invited, with Brother Max, to be an observer at the Vatican Council; he will take part in all the sessions through to 1965.
	December, visit to Taizé of Metropolitan Nikodim, of the Orthodox Patriarchate of Moscow.
1963	June, attends the Millennium celebrations at Mount Athos, Orthodox monastic centre.
1966	September, first international young adult meeting in Taizé; for the past several years, more and more young people had been coming.

1969	From now on there are Catholic brothers in the community.
1970	Easter, announcement of a "council of youth".
1973	May, first visit to Poland; speaks at the miners' pilgrimage in Piekary.
	September, the Archbishop of Canterbury, Dr Michael Ramsay, visits Taizé.
1974	April, in London, receives Templeton Prize for the progress of religion.
	August, opening of the Council of Youth; first letter to the young people, followed by one every year.
	October, in Frankfurt, German Booksellers' and Publishers' Peace Prize.
1975	Visit to Chile after the coup d'état; after this he will go every year to countries of the Southern hemisphere in difficult situations.
1976	Mother Teresa visits Taizé. Brother Roger goes to Kolkata to live alongside the very poor.
1978	June, visit to Russia.

	December, in Paris, first young adult European meeting, followed by one every year in a large European city, first in the West and then, from 1989, in the East as well.
1979	The Council of Youth is replaced by a pilgrimage which in 1985 will be called a "pilgrimage of trust on earth". The week-long meetings in Taizé last most of the year, from February to November.
1980	Young adult meetings in the USA (New York, Washington) and in Canada (Montreal, Ottawa, Toronto). Young adult meeting in East Germany. Young adult European meeting in Rome.
1982	Stay in Lebanon during the war there.
1983	Young adult meeting in Madrid. Visit to the US and USSR ambassadors. Mother Teresa in Taizé: joint call for solidarity and reconciliation.
1985	Together with children from every continent, Brother Roger brings the Secretary General of the United Nations, Javier Perez de Cuellar,

suggestions of the young for the UN to create trust among peoples.

December, first Asian meeting in Madras (India), with thousands of young adults from 45 countries.

1986   October 5, visit of Pope John Paul II to Taizé.
Young adult meetings in East Berlin and Warsaw.

1987   East-West young adult meeting in Ljubljana (Slovenia).
Young adult European meeting in Rome, with 24,000 participants including 5,000 from Eastern Europe.

1988   June, at the Millennium celebrations of the baptism of Russia in Moscow.
September, in Paris, UNESCO Prize for Peace Education.

1989   May, East-West young adult meeting in Pecs and Budapest (Hungary).
May, at Aachen, Germany, Charlemagne Prize: "The balance that Taizé seeks," said the jury, "can

be a model to end tensions in Europe, not just on a religious but also on a political level."

December, first young adult European meeting in Eastern Europe, at Wroclaw (Poland). with 50,000 participants.

1990　After the fall of the Berlin Wall, the number of young people coming to Taizé doubles; large narthexes are added to the Church of Reconciliation. Young adult meeting for Northern Europe in Linköping (Sweden).

1991　Young adult Asian meeting in Manila (Philippines).

1992　August, the Archbishop of Canterbury, Dr George Carey, spends a week in Taizé with a thousand young Anglicans.

September, Robert Schuman Prize awarded at Strasbourg, for Taizé's contribution to the building of Europe.

1994　May, visit of fourteen Swedish Lutheran bishops to Taizé.

1995	International meeting of young Africans in Johannesburg (South Africa).
1997	Speaks at the European Ecumenical Assembly in Graz (Austria).
1999	"Special guest" of the Synod on Europe in Rome.
2004	Animates for the last time a young adult European meeting, the 27th, in Lisbon.
2005	April 8, his last journey: to the funeral of Pope John Paul II in Rome. August 16, fatally attacked by a mentally disturbed assailant during evening prayer in the Church of Reconciliation in Taizé.

Captions of the photos
of the chronology

84/85
Brother Roger as a young man
Taizé years ago
Work
Prayer in the Romanesque church

86/87
The Council of Youth
Young people from all continents
Welcoming refugee children (Rwanda and Bosnia)

88/89
On the China Sea
In Kenya
In Haiti
In India

90/91
With... Pope John Paul II
...Patriarch Athenagoras of Constantinople
...Archbishop Ramsay of Canterbury
...the Swedish Lutheran bishops
Young adult European meeting

References to the texts

The texts of Brother Roger are short excerpts from his many publications, books or letters. They are not presented in chronological order but have been organized by topic. The ten chapters have been given titles that correspond to Brother Roger's most important books.

Here are the references to the texts chosen:

p. 25a and 81b: The Rule of Taizé, 1954 (in English 1961)

p. 16a and 17: The Dynamic of the Provisional, 1965 (1981)

p. 24: Festival, 1971 (1973)

p. 30: Struggle and Contemplation, 1973 (1974)

p. 10b, 31, 38a and 40: A Life we never Dared Hope For, 1976 (1981)

p. 25b and 52: The Wonder of a Love, 1979 (1981)

p. 12, 14, 16b, 20, 21, 28, 38c, 60 and 81a: Peace of Heart in All Things, 1995 (1996) & 2002 (2004)

p. 10a and 44: The Sources of Taizé, 2000

p. 49, 54 and 55 and the two flaps: God is Love Alone, 2003

p. 13, 32, 33, 38b, 70 and 77: Glimmers of Happiness 2005 (2007)

p. 22, 36, 42, 50, 66, 74 and 82: Praying in Silence of Heart – One Hundred Prayers, 2005 (2007)

(These last two published together in the UK under the title "A Path of Hope" 2006)

p. 62 and 63: Letter from Russia for 1989

p. 45: Letter "Astonished by Joy" for 2000

p. 68 and 72: Unfinished Letter for 2006

p. 80: Words of welcome for Pope John Paul II, Taizé, 5 October 1986

Photos:
Ciric: 90c
Wiesia Klemens: 91b
Kluba, editing.com: 11
Hans Lachmann: 86a, 88a, 88b,
Sabine Leutenegger: 6, 9, 12/13, 15, 18/19, 20/21, 23, 26/27, 29,
30/31, 37, 41, 43, 44, 48, 53, 56/57, 59, 64/65, 67, 69, 73, 75, 76,
78/79 and cover
Toni Schneiders: 85a
Taizé: 4, 34/35, 39, 46/47, 49, 61, 71, 83, 86b, 87, 89a, 89b, 91a, 134
D.R.: 84a, 84b, 85b, 90a, 90b

ISBN: 978-2-85040-310-1

© 2010 Ateliers et Presses de Taizé
71250 Taizé, France
tél. 03 85 50 30 30
community@taize.fr
www.taize.fr

DL juillet 2010 – N° 1118 – Les Presses de Taizé
imprimé en Allemagne